Whistle, Mary, Whistle...

Whistle, Mary, Whistle...

adapted by Bill Martin, Jr.
with pictures by Emanuele Luzzati
and handlettering by Ray Barber

HOLT, RINEHART AND WINSTON, INC.
New York   Toronto   London   Sydney

"*Whistle, Mary, whistle,
and you shall have a cow.*"

"I can't whistle, Mother,
because I don't know how."

"Whistle, Mary, whistle,
and you shall have a pig."

"I can't whistle, Mother,
because I'm not so big."

"*Whistle, Mary, whistle,*
and you shall have a sheep."

"I can't whistle, Mother,
because I am asleep."

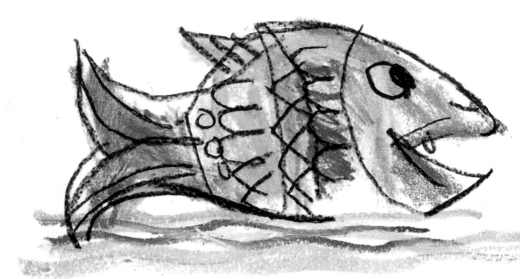

"*Whistle, Mary, whistle,
and you shall have a trout.*"

"I can't whistle, Mother,
because my tooth is out."

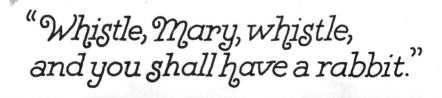

"Whistle, Mary, whistle,
and you shall have a rabbit."

"I can't whistle, Mother,
because I've lost the habit."

"Whistle, Mary, whistle,
and you shall have a goat."

"I can't whistle, Mother,
because it hurts my throat."

"Whistle, Mary, whistle,
and you shall have a daisy."

"I can't whistle, Mother,
because it looks so crazy."

*"Whistle, Mary, whistle,
and you shall have a pickle."*

"I can't whistle, Mother,
because it makes me tickle."

"*Whistle, Mary, whistle, and you shall have some honey.*"

"I can't whistle, Mother,
because it feels so funny."

"Whistle, Mary, whistle,
and you shall have some bread."

"I can't whistle, Mother,
because I'm standing on my head."

"Whistle, Mary, whistle,
and you shall have a pie."

"I can't whistle, Mother,
because my mouth is dry."

"Whistle, Mary, whistle,
and you shall have some gold."

"I can't whistle, Mother,
because I'm not that old."

"Whistle, Mary, whistle,
and you shall have the moon."

"I can't whistle, Mother,
because I've lost the tune."

"Tweet, tweeet, tweeeet, tweeeee

"Whistle, Mary, whistle,
and you shall have a man."

eet,
tweeeeeet,
I just found out I can."